Poems From A Grumpy Old Man

Ash Carlton

BookLeaf Publishing

India | USA | UK

Presentation by *BookLeaf Publishing*

Web: www.bookleafpub.com

E-mail: info@bookleafpub.com

ISBN: 9789358737394

First edition 2023

power of dreams has shown me that there are no limits to the worlds we can create with words.

As I embark on this poetic journey, I carry your love, your spirit, and your inspiration with me every step of the way. My words are a testament to the profound impact you have had on my life, and the world is a more beautiful place because of you.

Thank you, my dear son and daughter, for being my muses, my guiding stars, and my greatest treasures. I dedicate my poetry to you, with all the love in my heart.

Forever yours,

Pops

To my beloved son and daughter,

You are the radiant stars that have illuminated the skies of my life, filling every moment with love, joy, and boundless inspiration. It is with the deepest gratitude and an overflowing heart that I dedicate my poetic journey to you both.

From the very first moment I held you in my arms, I knew that you were my muses, my guiding lights, my eternal sources of creativity. Your laughter, your innocence, your dreams – they have all ignited the flames of imagination within me, fueling the words that flow from my soul onto the pages of my poems.

In your smiles, I find the sunshine that brightens my verses. In your curiosity, I discover the endless questions that beckon me to explore the depths of thought. In your love, I encounter the boundless wellspring of emotions that breathe life into my lines.

You have taught me the beauty of simplicity, the magic in the mundane, and the wonder in the world around us. Your unwavering belief in the

PREFACE

In the digital age, where countless voices clamor for our attention and the rapid pace of life often leaves us feeling disconnected from the world around us, poetry remains a timeless refuge—a sanctuary of words that can transport us to another time, another place, and another state of mind. It's within the embrace of poetry that we rediscover the power of language to awaken our senses, provoke introspection, and inspire profound emotions.

The poems in this collection, drawn from the virtual pages of "Grumpy Old Man Poetry," offer readers a glimpse into the unique and unfiltered perspective of their author, a self-proclaimed "grumpy old man." Yet, beyond the gruff exterior lies a wealth of wisdom, insight, and an unapologetic passion for life, nature, and the human experience.

In an era when many voices are lost in the digital cacophony, these poems stand as a testament to the enduring relevance of the written word and the eternal longing of the human soul to express itself through language. Each poem, a carefully crafted snapshot of a moment in time or a journey of the heart, invites us to pause, reflect, and connect with the thoughts and emotions that define our shared humanity.

As you embark on this poetic journey, I encourage you to let go of the distractions of the digital world, if only for a moment, and immerse yourself in the vivid imagery, poignant reflections, and raw emotions that these verses evoke. Whether you find solace, inspiration, or simply a moment of respite within these pages, know that you are not alone in your quest to make sense of the world and to find beauty in its often chaotic tapestry.

Poetry, after all, is a timeless conversation—a dialogue between the poet and the reader, and, ultimately, a reflection of the human condition. As we delve into the grumpy old man's world of words, may we find in his poetry a mirror for our own experiences, a source of inspiration, and a reminder that, no matter how grumpy life may sometimes seem, there is always room for beauty, wonder, and connection.

So, turn the page and let the grumpy old man's words wash over you. Allow his poems to transport you, challenge you, and perhaps even make you smile. For in these verses, you may discover a bit of yourself and a glimpse of the world through the eyes of a grumpy old man who, in his own way, has found solace and meaning in the art of poetry.

Brother Billy

As we look, heads raised, toward the sky.
The thought of you brings a tear to our eye.
Mixed are the tears of laughter and pain.
Knowing in this life we won't see you again.
We listen to the music that made you sing.
Trusting that God has placed you on wing.
Another angel he now has today.
You've headed home in your own way.
Never turn off a good song until it's over.
We all wait to see you again in a field of clover.
You've touched us all with the size of your heart.
Your memory from us will never part.
You were loud, stern, and sometimes silly.
Blood or not, we'll miss you, Billy.

My Other Mom

She wasn't mine, but I called her mom.
Hearing her voice for the spirit is a balm.
She raised my friends, no, my sister and
brothers.
I'm glad to say I've had two great mothers.
She lies there holding hands with dad.
Remembering the wonderful life together
they've had.
All the happiness and joy, the sorrow and tears.
A guiding light to the family throughout the
years.
She raised four sons and a daughter with love.
All the while worshiping the lord above.
She's all smiles and humor though her time
draws near.
Around the room on every face sits a tear.
Two sons wait to see and hug her again.
Soon our wait to see her will begin.

The Kiss

Lunch was over and it's hard to believe.
An hour was spent and it's time to leave.
Out to the parking lot we go.
Mutual happiness making both glow.

My heart continues to race.
All from the excitement of the chase.
We hug, say goodbye, and step back.
I reach out for her but this is no attack.

I pull her into my arms and give her our first.
Our lips touch and all others are now the worst.
This is our love at its start.
Way too soon we must part.

Now there's a smile on each face.
But soon we must leave this place.
More goodbyes are said
To our cars, we both start to head.

Looking back I see her jump and click her heels.
Landing she turns to me, her smile full of feels.
My smile for her is something I cannot hide.
For this is the only woman I want by my side.

Mourning

It is always a sad time when we lose a loved
one.
We feel anguish as there's nothing to be done.
Save remembering what they created in our life.
With memories so full of happiness and strife.
Just know they now rest in a much better place.
So be at ease and keep a smile upon your face.
For now, you must endure heartache and pain.
Take comfort in the fact you will see them again.

Cat's Lunch

I watch her black form sway with a slow wiggle.
Sitting in the grass I watch and suppress a
giggle.
Wide green eyes focused and fully aware.
The grasshopper is ignorant of her stare.
Her black tail used for balance is stiff and
straight.
There is but a moment left according to fate.
Muscles tense and twitch as they prepare.
Instantly she launches herself into the air.
The grasshopper tries but gets caught
underneath.
It now has no escape from the cat's teeth.

True Love

You see them walking in, coming as a pair.
Their love can be seen in their stare.
Each holding the other's hand.
Whether or not they sit or stand.
Together they whisper and giggle.
His kiss on her cheek makes her wiggle.
They both talk about their first house.
Glad they are to be the other's spouse.
Each day they get a little older.
I love you, every day he makes sure he's told her.
Gentle is the kiss he placed on her forehead.
Each evening, each goes to their bed.
Nurses tuck them in for a night's rest.
They remember their lives as being the best.

Together

Hand in hand together they walk.
Sweetness is the language they talk.
He is her world and she is his.
She is the answer to his life's quiz.
They complete each other's life.
He, her husband and she, his wife.

When You Are

When you are tired, take my energy.
Because together we have synergy.
When you are weak, take my strength.
How long you need it, it doesn't matter the
length.
When you are lonely, take my hand.
Beside you, I will gladly stand.
When you are scared, take my arm.
I will protect you from all harm.
When you are just, you, take my heart.
For that is the best part of you, from that I will
never part.

Love Of All

You were born different than I.
Those differences are more than meet the eye.
Whether you are straight or gay.
It matters not to me I will say.
You are the person that stands before me.
No matter if you want to be called he or she.
I realize I am not to judge.
On this fact, others wouldn't budge.
It truly matters not to me.
Who another chooses to be.
We all basically want the same thing.
To be wanted and loved by another human
being.
Some people are set in their way.
Yet others change with a new day.
I have said things that were ugly and that hurt.
Knowing I've done so makes me feel lower than
dirt.
For some that pain I can never take away.
I'm so sorry for the things I made the mistake to
say.

A Day In The Life

What a great day it is starting out to be.
Only soft white clouds in the sky to see.
A day like today makes your steps light.
Seeing friendly faces with eyes so bright.
Some people wave as others kindly smile.
The beauty of this day grows for a while.
A soft memory of one you used to know.
Brightness fades, the dark starts to grow.
Her memory creeps in your mind to stay.
Clouds start to gather, ruining your day.
Nothing more than echoes, beautiful face.
Skip of your heart and slowing your pace.
Soon those heavy gates are bursting wide.
Pouring out memories once locked inside.
It's hard to be stand up tall and be a man.
As you fight back tears as hard as you can.
All those emotions being a constant strain.
None know because you hide all the pain.
Behind the wheel, you wait on the green.
Deciphering what the things said, do mean.
There are none with whom you can share.
Even from mouths of promise, none care.
Your two hearts apart for many long years.
Apart from you, none understand the tears.
So, you are left to suffer quietly and alone.
Just you and memories of one that's gone.

Emptiness

I try to breathe but the air seems thick.
I sit trying to figure out what makes me tick.
It's not enough to wonder why.
I turn my head towards the sky.
I plead with God, what can I do.
I need to know so I can find you.
Maybe we've met then again maybe not.
I just want to love and be loved with all we've
got.
Time drags on each and every day.
Making me wonder and begin again to pray.

Pup

On my lap, she is curled up.
My red beagle, my little pup.
She sits there after a hard day.
All worn out from so much play.
With a twitch and a relaxed sigh,
She snuggles against my thigh.
Her comfort is a pleasure to my sight.
To have this little pup is pure delight.

My Grandma

You're the only one I have ever known.
From a child, to now being fully grown.
Always you were there with a smile.
Even though weary from each mile.
On your lips, was always a favorite song.
Yet quick to correct when I'd done wrong.
Like when I let that hammer hit my head.
And up the steps I went, seeing only red.
In shock and fear I knocked on the door.
Scared I'd get blood on the kitchen floor.
On the counter I sat, you stroking my hair.
I realized a bloody flood was never a care.
Always with kindness and love, you did it all.
From cooking macaroni to going to the mall.
I remember this and more with a teary eye.
As with friends and family, we say goodbye.
Today a celebration of the wonderful life,
Of the one called Mom, Grandma, and Wife.

Armor

There's heavy armor upon my heart.
Protecting me by doing its part.
Little by little it's been placed there.
Added by those who didn't care.
With a clunk, each found its place.
Placed by those with a smiling face.
Then a little witch I did meet.
Now a pile of armor lies at her feet.
With a heart that is now laid bare.
Thinking only of the life I wish to share.
For it was her arrow that was in my heart.
Not ending life, but giving love a start.

When Knight Falls

One by one each knight had to fall.
Each summoned Home by the call.
Fellow knights thus called to His side.
As we stand with tears yet undried.
They wore black and orange in life.
Now they rest, suffering no more strife.
Our friends and family have been lost.
Each one has paid the ultimate cost.
Now left behind, we do miss our friends.
Awaiting our turn for when this life ends.
To stand with those for whom we've cried.
Forever full of Black Knight pride.

This poem was written for those who went to my
high school and unfortunately passed away. This
was my way of honoring them and helping
others who are grieving the loss of a loved one.

Red Thread

What does the Red Thread mean to me?
It's something very special as you will see.
It's about two soul mates and one love.
About a love that others will be jealous of.
It's red, for the blood coursing through my heart.
Blood from which, to keep them safe, I'd gladly
part.
It's a thread, two soul mates together it does
bind.
From one little finger to another, it will wind.
It's red, to symbolize love.
Second only to that which comes from above.
It's a thread, to repair the cracks in a broken
heart.
Binding pieces together so they'll never again
part.

For She Is The Reason That I'm Here

For she is the reason that I'm here,
There is nothing in Hell I will fear.
I gaze through the gates at all of them.
Mangled demons, commanded by him.
Each a visage of anger and rage.
As each fights to leave this cage.

For she is the reason that I'm here,
There is nothing in Hell I will fear.
I see her there, crumpled upon that hill.
Her fading light fills my heart with a chill.
Forward I step with just a simple task.
To protect and within her love to bask.

For she is the reason that I'm here,
There is nothing in Hell I will fear.
The reason she's here I do not know.
By her side, I'm called and hastily go.
Not weak, she's a victim of another's harm.
Too proud to ask, forever she has my arm.

For she is the reason that I'm here,
There is nothing in Hell I will fear.
With hands heaving upon the gate,

It's flung asunder from pent-up hate.
Releasing wails to make me flinch,
From my smile, backward they inch.

For she is the reason that I'm here,
There is nothing in Hell I will fear.
As I stroll through the gates of Hell,
Foul is the odor, brimstone I smell.
In others, fear would begin to grow.
Onward I tread with none to show.

For she is the reason that I'm here,
There is nothing in Hell I will fear.
For me, they grasp with jagged claws.
Pulling toward sharp gnashing maws.
Each reaching to tear or devour my soul.
All desiring me to remain within this hole.

For she is the reason that I'm here,
There is nothing in Hell I will fear.
Forward I step, with no reason for to dwell
Yet in others, fear would grow and swell.
Maybe it's her test or maybe mine?
As I'll walk amongst my future kind.

For she is the reason that I'm here,
There is nothing in Hell I will fear.
My past sins coalescing into a spiny chain.
Around limbs, for control, and causing pain.

To her, I progress and chains do break.
My resolve these demons will not shake.

For she is the reason that I'm here,
There is nothing in Hell I will fear.
At her side, I freeze, stopped by the blood.
Both her wings lying beside her in the mud.
In my arms, I take her over shrieking jeers.
Head on my chest, mingling are our tears.

For she is the reason that I'm here,
There is nothing in Hell I will fear.
Now safe in my arms, to Hell's gate I head.
She must leave this land of burning dead.
Back through the gauntlet, I go again.
To the Hell's gate where this all began.

For she is the reason that I'm here,
There is nothing in Hell I will fear.
Steps past the gate, with a soft sweet voice,
"I'm sorry," she says as if I had any choice.
The sound of her voice easing my own pain.
"For you, my love, it's all worth doing again."

For she is the reason that I'm here,
There is nothing in Hell I will fear.
On soft green grass, I place her at His feet.
Forehead kiss as a goodbye, then retreat.
Never again to fly, forever to walk the earth.
My angel will never know, to me her worth.

For He Is The Reason That I'm Here

For he is the reason that I'm here,
He's eviler than all Hell that I fear.
I see him, standing tall upon the ground.
Seeing me, unlike the others all around.
There was a kindness within his smile.
Resting my wings, we talk for a while.

For he is the reason that I'm here,
He's eviler than all Hell that I fear.
I was innocent and new to the wing.
Words of love, to woo me he'd sing.
Pleasure was found within his voice.
To listen for hours, always my choice.

For he is the reason that I'm here,
He's eviler than all Hell that I fear.
His words, sweet, strong, and new.
From that within, a new love grew.
The first of my many, I love each one.
To his side, without pause, I must run.

For he is the reason that I'm here,
He's eviler than all Hell that I fear.
Slowly words began to sting a bit.

Trying for his smile, I must not quit.
Sharp words, to bring some pain.
Then hollow promises of not again.

For he is the reason that I'm here,
He's eviler than all Hell that I fear.
Now his fist, my back against the wall.
One by one my feathers began to fall.
Too late those horns I would see.
Life or wing, one he'd take from me.

For he is the reason that I'm here,
He's eviler than all Hell that I fear.
Long years I would suffer and plead.
My pain was his overwhelming need.
To save mine, I try to flee but can't go.
My punishment, the world he will show.

For he is the reason that I'm here,
He's eviler than all Hell that I fear.
Force of will and powered by hate.
My wings and I, he does separate.
Pain and horror, causing his glee.
Vision dims and the dark takes me.

For he is the reason that I'm here,
He's eviler than all Hell that I fear.
With fluttering eyes again I can see.
A red thread leading away from me.

To a man standing at Hell's gate.
Within him, I feel love, not hate.

For he is the reason that I'm here,
He's eviler than all Hell that I fear.
Pain again, into the dark I fall away.
Soon to awake from a gentle sway.
Within chained arms, I'm carried I see.
A red thread leading from him to me.

For he is the reason that I'm here,
He's eviler than all Hell that I fear.
Protection I feel in his loving embrace.
Carrying me from this wretched place.
My head on his chest and mingling of tears.
I feel safer than I have in many long years.

For he is the reason that I'm here,
He's eviler than all Hell that I fear.
Through Hell's gate, he carries me at last.
Shame fills me with worry about my past.
"I'm sorry" I struggle to say through the pain.
"For you, my love, it's all worth doing again."

For he is the reason that I'm here,
He's eviler than all Hell that I fear.
At the master's feet, I'm placed at long last.
A soft forehead kiss and he's gone too fast.
Beyond the gate he goes, then his back I see.
More tears well up, scars where mine will be.

Talking With The Wind

Standing high upon the mountain peak.
With my lungs full of anger, I firmly begin.
To the air and the ether aloud I speak.
Words joined with the roaring of the wind.

"Try your best and try with all your might."
"Nothing will change and we'll only grow."
To the universe I say, be it day or night.
"This is something that all must know."

"With pride I am hers and she is mine."
"Throw what you will and throw it hard."
"We will choose each other each time."
"It matters not if our flesh gets scared."

"For it is our spirits we both hold dear"
The wind howled, increasing in rage.
The galeforce faded, and the air clear.
"I've known you both for more than an age."

"Both of you I have watched since birth."
"You have cared and longed for another,"
"But, none have ever seen your worth."
"Yet there's only ever been one lover."

"The trials and tribulations were a must"
"To show you what the other means to you."
"Both now know the other holds your trust."
"Take comfort in finding a love so true."

"Know your love and ours are the same."
"Cherish each other like none in the past."
"Hold each other's hand with no shame."
"For this is not just a love, but one to last."

"Know that around your finger is a thread."
"One we placed there so long ago."
"It symbolizes your love, a color so red."
"Leading to one only a heart would know."

I left the mountaintop, my rage being spent.
To a little cottage as if from a fantasy tome.
And to the loving arms I hold so dear, I went.
Knowing with a kiss, my heart was home.

Visions Of The Future

When I look into your eyes I can see our future.
A Saturday spent vegetable picking at the local
farmer's market.
Finding the perfect colors to match the nursery's
carpet.
When you've spent all night sick and I'm helping
you into the shower.
Seeing you watch me from the window as I plant
your favorite flower.
The fight we'll have where we didn't talk for a
couple of days.
Us sitting watching the sun slowly remove the
morning's haze.
The food fight while making Saturday dinner
with the kids on their way.
Slow dancing in the same kitchen with the only
reason, it's Tuesday.
Better yet, when I look into the future I can see
your eyes.

The Three Pats

Love is full of lots of little this and thats.
But do you know about the Three Pats?
So simple, a quick one, two, and a third.
To convey one's thoughts without a word.
Given with a hug as to comfort a sad tear.
Or as a simple, never be in doubt my dear.
They may be given any time or place.
In the dead of night or during an embrace.
The first stands for the giver, it's the I.
As soft as the softest, contented sigh.
The second, a heart that is full it's love.
Given to one freely with never a shove.
Lastly, take it to heart, meaning is you.
What is being said is honest and true.
I told you this to be sure that you knew.
Three Pats say without saying…

I love you